I LOVE MY PLANTS

A Gardening Journal

RP STUDIO

PHILADELPHIA

RP Studio
Hachette Book Group
1290 Avenue of the Americas, New York, NY 10104
www.runningpress.com
@Running_Press

Printed in China

First Edition: February 2020

Published by RP Studio, an imprint of Perseus Books, LLC, a subsidiary of Hachette Book Group, Inc. The RP Studio name and logo is a trademark of the Hachette Book Group.

The publisher is not responsible for websites (or their content) that are not owned by the publisher.

Text by Claire Wallace

Design by Jenna McBride

ISBN: 978-0-7624-6802-7

RRD-S

10 9 8 7 6 5 4 3 2 1

Introduction

Plants are a simple, easy way to brighten up a living space or outdoor area. Many plants purify the air by removing toxins, and studies have shown that having plants in your home or workplace can lower stress levels and make you feel more relaxed. Basically, plants make people happy!

Some of the easiest plants to take care of are succulents and cacti. Most succulents and cacti can go long stretches of time without water, which makes them a great choice for someone who travels a lot or just tends to forget about their plants. As a rule of thumb, you should wait until the soil is dry or almost dry before watering succulents and cacti, although this will vary somewhat depending on what type of plant you have and how dry the air is. The one thing succulents and cacti do need is plenty of sunlight, though, so make sure they're near a window that gets enough sun.

Houseplants require somewhat more care than succulents and cacti, but they're well worth it for their aesthetic and air-cleansing properties. Most houseplants need to be

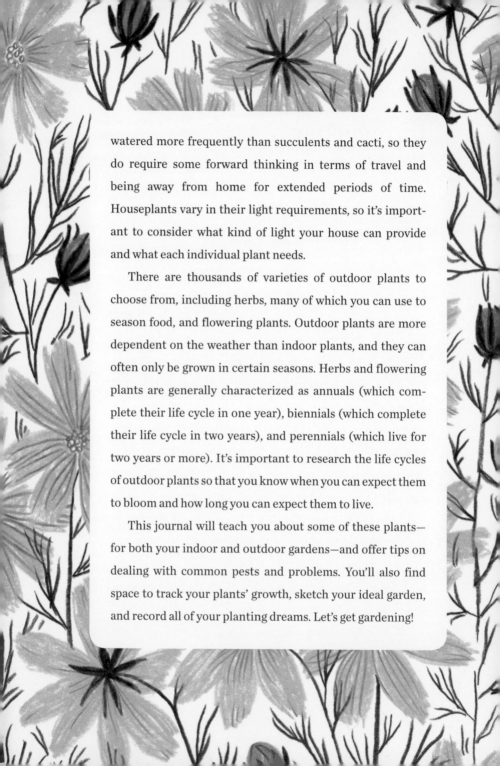

watered more frequently than succulents and cacti, so they do require some forward thinking in terms of travel and being away from home for extended periods of time. Houseplants vary in their light requirements, so it's important to consider what kind of light your house can provide and what each individual plant needs.

There are thousands of varieties of outdoor plants to choose from, including herbs, many of which you can use to season food, and flowering plants. Outdoor plants are more dependent on the weather than indoor plants, and they can often only be grown in certain seasons. Herbs and flowering plants are generally characterized as annuals (which complete their life cycle in one year), biennials (which complete their life cycle in two years), and perennials (which live for two years or more). It's important to research the life cycles of outdoor plants so that you know when you can expect them to bloom and how long you can expect them to live.

This journal will teach you about some of these plants—for both your indoor and outdoor gardens—and offer tips on dealing with common pests and problems. You'll also find space to track your plants' growth, sketch your ideal garden, and record all of your planting dreams. Let's get gardening!

INDOOR PLANTS

Spider Plants

Native to South Africa, spider plants (*Chlorophytum comosum*), also called airplane plants and ribbon plants, are grown all over the world. They have long, thin, ribbon-like leaves, which arch up and out from the center. The leaves are either fully green or, in the case of the variegated variety, green with a white stripe in the center, and they can produce white flowers in the summer. Spider plants are adaptable, fast-growing, and easy to care for, so they're a great choice for beginners. They're also very easy to propagate, or breed from a parent plant, because they do it on their own: spider plants produce smaller versions of themselves, called pups. Once the pups have grown roots, they can be removed from the larger plant and planted in their own pots.

LIGHT

Spider plants tend to like bright or moderate indirect sunlight; direct sunlight can scorch their leaves. They can survive in lower light, but they might not produce as many pups. Variegated spider plants, which are white and green, may become fully green in lower light.

WATER +SOIL

Spider plants like a moderate amount of moisture. They don't like to be too wet, but you shouldn't let the soil dry out entirely. Plant in a well-draining soil to avoid root rot, and don't pour water directly into the center of the plant. Depending on the humidity level of your house and how quickly the soil dries out, you should plan to water your spider plants once every week or two.

ⓘ **OTHER INFO**

It's fairly common for the tips of spider plants to turn brown, which is often a result of too much fluoride or salt in the water, or too little moisture. Use distilled water to keep the tips from browning, and don't let the soil dry out entirely between watering. You can cut off any tips that do turn brown.

Umbrella Plants

Umbrella plants, which have floppy leaves that somewhat resemble umbrellas, can grow up to six feet tall indoors (and, in the right conditions, over forty feet tall outdoors!), so they're great if you're looking for a low-maintenance, attractive focal point for an indoor space. Over time, the lower leaves can fall off the plant, leaving only a canopy of leaves at the top. There are actually two different types of umbrella plants: the umbrella tree, *Schefflera actinophylla*, and the smaller *Schefflera arboricola*, often called the dwarf umbrella tree.

LIGHT

Umbrella plants like moderate or bright indirect light. They can survive in lower light, although they may become somewhat leggy as they stretch to reach the light. Avoid placing the plants in direct sunlight, which can cause their leaves to burn.

WATER +SOIL

Umbrella plants tend to grow well in moist soil. Overwatering can lead to root rot, so make sure the soil has dried out somewhat before watering again, but try not to let the soil dry out entirely.

OTHER INFO

Umbrella plants can grow very tall if they're given adequate water and food and are grown in the right light conditions. However, if you'd prefer a shorter, smaller plant, you can prune the shoots near the top of the plant, which will encourage more growth closer to the base.

Snake Plants

The snake plant (*Sansevieria trifasciata*), also known as mother-in-law's tongue, is one of the easiest indoor plants to care for because it can survive in low light and doesn't need much water. Native to tropical Africa, the plant has long, snake-like green leaves that can grow up to eight feet high. A snake plant can be easily propagated by cutting off a few inches of one of its leaves and putting it in soil, or by dividing the plant at its base.

LIGHT

Snake plants prefer moderate light, but they can survive in a variety of light conditions, including low light, making them ideal for darker corners that need brightening up.

WATER +SOIL

Snake plants do not need—or want—a lot of water. You should water them once every few weeks or even less, depending on how much humidity is in the air where you live. Let the soil dry out before watering them again, and use a well-draining soil, because too much water can lead to root rot.

OTHER INFO

One downside to snake plants is that they're mildly toxic to cats or dogs. If you have pets, make sure to keep these plants out of reach.

Jade

Jade plants (*Crassula ovata*) are succulents, which means they don't need to be watered very frequently because they store water in their leaves and stems. Native to South Africa, jade plants have dark green leaves and thick brown stems that can resemble small tree trunks. If cared for properly, jade can live for a very long time. They're also easy to propagate, using either cuttings or leaves, which means they can easily be shared with family and friends.

LIGHT

Jades like bright light. They can survive with less light, but they may become leggy, as the leaves stretch to reach the sun.

WATER +SOIL

Like most succulents, jades don't need to be watered as often as other houseplants, but you shouldn't let the soil dry out completely before watering. Depending on humidity levels, jade plants typically like to be watered every week or two.

OTHER INFO

Jade leaves are usually dark green, but their edges may become red if exposed to bright sunlight. The flowers produced by jade plants are particularly nice: they look like tiny white or pink stars.

Pothos

Pothos plants (*Epipremnum aureum*) are popular houseplants because of their attractive, trailing heart-shaped leaves and their ability to survive in low light. They don't require a lot of work to maintain, and they can tolerate a variety of light conditions. A lot of people put them on high shelves, because they can get long: outdoors, in the right conditions, pothos can grow to forty feet or more, though they likely won't grow to more than eight or ten feet indoors in containers.

LIGHT

Pothos plants like moderate light, but they can survive in low light, making them a good choice for offices and even bathrooms.

WATER +SOIL

You should water your pothos once every week or two. Don't let the soil dry out entirely.

OTHER INFO

Pothos plants are somewhat toxic to humans and animals if ingested, so keep them away from pets and children (and don't eat them yourself!). Pothos can grow in either soil or water, and are easily propagated by taking a cutting, stripping the leaves from the bottom few inches of the stem (closest to where it was cut), and placing the stem in either soil or water.

COMMON PROBLEMS WITH INDOOR PLANTS

Root or stem rot. Root or stem rot is one of the most common causes of plant death. It's caused by overwatering, or by allowing a plant to sit in water. To avoid root rot, make sure you don't water too often, and use a well-draining soil so that your plant isn't sitting in liquid. You should also make sure that your pots have drainage holes, which allow excess water to drain out. If you have a saucer underneath your pot, make sure to discard any excess liquid that collects after watering.

Root bound plants. A plant is considered root bound when its roots have grown to fill the pot and can't expand any further. When the roots can't expand, they can't get enough nutrients, which will often cause the plant to stop growing, and may even cause it to wilt and eventually die. If your plant has stopped growing or has started to wilt, you should consider whether it needs to be repotted in a larger container. If you take the plant out of its pot and see that the roots take up almost all the space, with very little room for soil, you should repot the plant in a larger pot. In general, most plants should be repotted every year or two so that they don't become root bound.

Leggy plants. Plants may become leggy when they don't get enough light, because the plant stretches to reach what light there is. Often plants that become overly leggy end up drooping, because the stems are too long and thin to support the weight of the leaves. To prevent your plants from becoming too leggy, make sure they're exposed to adequate light.

Mold. Mold can affect both indoor and outdoor plants. It's often a result of overwatering, or too much humidity. Mold won't always kill a plant, but it could slow the plant's growth. It's unattractive, and it can sometimes be an indication that the growing conditions aren't ideal. Your plant may also be in danger of pests or root rot. To avoid mold, make sure you're not overwatering your plant or letting it sit in water, and make sure the humidity level isn't too high. You should use a well-draining soil, as well as a pot with drainage holes, and you should remove any rotten or damaged leaves or stems. If mold does grow on the soil, you can try scraping it off, or repotting your plant in fresh soil.

Leaf spots. Black or brown spots on leaves often indicate a bacteria or fungus. Bacteria and fungi can't always be avoided, but you can try to prevent them by keeping leaves dry and not overwatering plants or letting them sit in water. You should remove any affected leaves as soon as possible.

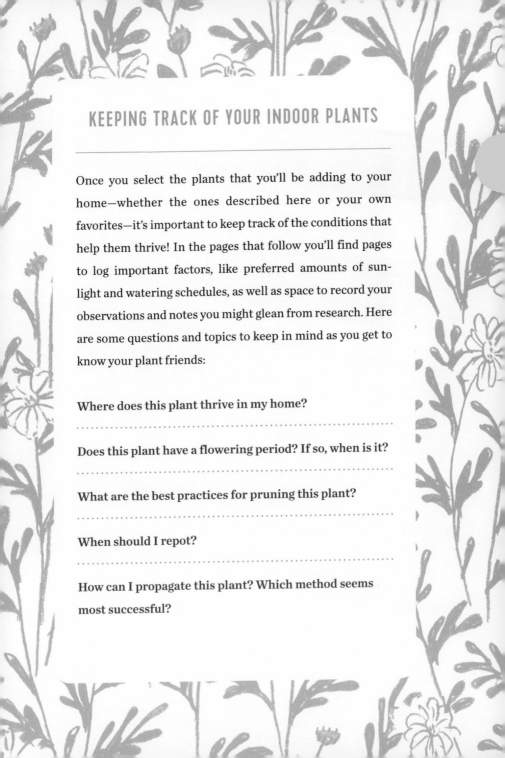

KEEPING TRACK OF YOUR INDOOR PLANTS

Once you select the plants that you'll be adding to your home—whether the ones described here or your own favorites—it's important to keep track of the conditions that help them thrive! In the pages that follow you'll find pages to log important factors, like preferred amounts of sunlight and watering schedules, as well as space to record your observations and notes you might glean from research. Here are some questions and topics to keep in mind as you get to know your plant friends:

Where does this plant thrive in my home?
....

Does this plant have a flowering period? If so, when is it?
....

What are the best practices for pruning this plant?
....

When should I repot?
....

How can I propagate this plant? Which method seems most successful?

PLANT NAME:

SUNLIGHT

LEVEL OF SUNLIGHT:
○ LOW ◐ BRIGHT / INDIRECT ◑ PARTIAL / DIRECT ● DIRECT

THRIVES IN THIS LOCATION: _____

_____

_____

WATER

AMOUNT:
☐ LET DRY OUT ☐ MIST ☐ KEEP DAMP ☐ SOAK

FREQUENCY:
☐ 2–3X WEEK ☐ 1–2X WEEK ☐ WEEKLY ☐ BI-WEEKLY ☐ MONTHLY

WATER ON:
☐ MON ☐ TUE ☐ WED ☐ THU ☐ FRI ☐ SAT ☐ SUN

SOIL

TYPE OF SOIL: _____

_____

PREFERRED BRAND: _____

_____

FERTILIZER

TYPE OF FERTILIZER: _____

PREFERRED BRAND: _____

_____

FREQUENCY OF USE: _____

ADDITIONAL CARE NOTES

• • •

PLANT NAME:

SUNLIGHT

LEVEL OF SUNLIGHT:
○ LOW   ◐ BRIGHT / INDIRECT   ◑ PARTIAL / DIRECT   ● DIRECT

THRIVES IN THIS LOCATION: _____

_____

_____

WATER

AMOUNT:
☐ LET DRY OUT   ☐ MIST   ☐ KEEP DAMP   ☐ SOAK

FREQUENCY:
☐ 2–3X WEEK   ☐ 1–2X WEEK   ☐ WEEKLY   ☐ BI-WEEKLY   ☐ MONTHLY

WATER ON:
☐ MON   ☐ TUE   ☐ WED   ☐ THU   ☐ FRI   ☐ SAT   ☐ SUN

SOIL

TYPE OF SOIL: _____

_____

_____

PREFERRED BRAND: _____

_____

FERTILIZER

TYPE OF FERTILIZER: _____

_____

PREFERRED BRAND: _____

_____

FREQUENCY OF USE: _____

ADDITIONAL CARE NOTES

_____
_____
_____
_____
_____
_____
_____
_____
_____
_____
_____
_____
_____
_____
_____
_____
_____
_____
_____
_____
_____
_____

• • •

PLANT NAME:

SUNLIGHT

LEVEL OF SUNLIGHT:
◯ LOW ◑ BRIGHT / INDIRECT ◑ PARTIAL / DIRECT ⬤ DIRECT

THRIVES IN THIS LOCATION: _____
_____
_____

WATER

AMOUNT:
☐ LET DRY OUT ☐ MIST ☐ KEEP DAMP ☐ SOAK

FREQUENCY:
☐ 2–3X WEEK ☐ 1–2X WEEK ☐ WEEKLY ☐ BI-WEEKLY ☐ MONTHLY

WATER ON:
☐ MON ☐ TUE ☐ WED ☐ THU ☐ FRI ☐ SAT ☐ SUN

SOIL

TYPE OF SOIL: _____
_____
_____

PREFERRED BRAND: _____
_____

FERTILIZER

TYPE OF FERTILIZER: _____

PREFERRED BRAND: _____

_____

FREQUENCY OF USE: _____

ADDITIONAL CARE NOTES

_____
_____
_____
_____
_____
_____
_____
_____
_____
_____
_____
_____
_____
_____
_____
_____
_____
_____
_____
_____
_____
_____
_____

• • •

PLANT NAME:

SUNLIGHT

LEVEL OF SUNLIGHT:
○ LOW ◗ BRIGHT / INDIRECT ◑ PARTIAL / DIRECT ● DIRECT

THRIVES IN THIS LOCATION: _____
_____
_____

WATER

AMOUNT:
☐ LET DRY OUT ☐ MIST ☐ KEEP DAMP ☐ SOAK

FREQUENCY:
☐ 2–3X WEEK ☐ 1–2X WEEK ☐ WEEKLY ☐ BI-WEEKLY ☐ MONTHLY

WATER ON:
☐ MON ☐ TUE ☐ WED ☐ THU ☐ FRI ☐ SAT ☐ SUN

SOIL

TYPE OF SOIL: _____
_____
_____

PREFERRED BRAND: _____
_____

FERTILIZER

TYPE OF FERTILIZER: _____

PREFERRED BRAND: _____

FREQUENCY OF USE: _____

ADDITIONAL CARE NOTES

_____
_____
_____
_____
_____
_____
_____
_____
_____
_____
_____
_____
_____
_____
_____
_____
_____
_____
_____
_____
_____
_____

• • •

PLANT LOG

PLANT NAME:

SUNLIGHT

LEVEL OF SUNLIGHT:
○ LOW ◑ BRIGHT / INDIRECT ◐ PARTIAL / DIRECT ● DIRECT

THRIVES IN THIS LOCATION: _____
_____
_____

WATER

AMOUNT:
☐ LET DRY OUT ☐ MIST ☐ KEEP DAMP ☐ SOAK

FREQUENCY:
☐ 2–3X WEEK ☐ 1–2X WEEK ☐ WEEKLY ☐ BI-WEEKLY ☐ MONTHLY

WATER ON:
☐ MON ☐ TUE ☐ WED ☐ THU ☐ FRI ☐ SAT ☐ SUN

SOIL

TYPE OF SOIL: _____
_____
_____

PREFERRED BRAND: _____
_____

FERTILIZER

TYPE OF FERTILIZER: _____
_____

PREFERRED BRAND: _____
_____

FREQUENCY OF USE: _____

ADDITIONAL CARE NOTES

· · ·

PLANT LOG

PLANT NAME:

SUNLIGHT

LEVEL OF SUNLIGHT:
○ LOW ◐ BRIGHT / INDIRECT ◑ PARTIAL / DIRECT ● DIRECT

THRIVES IN THIS LOCATION: _____

_____

_____

WATER

AMOUNT:
☐ LET DRY OUT ☐ MIST ☐ KEEP DAMP ☐ SOAK

FREQUENCY:
☐ 2–3X WEEK ☐ 1–2X WEEK ☐ WEEKLY ☐ BI-WEEKLY ☐ MONTHLY

WATER ON:
☐ MON ☐ TUE ☐ WED ☐ THU ☐ FRI ☐ SAT ☐ SUN

SOIL

TYPE OF SOIL: _____

_____

PREFERRED BRAND: _____

_____

FERTILIZER

TYPE OF FERTILIZER: _____

PREFERRED BRAND: _____

FREQUENCY OF USE: _____

ADDITIONAL CARE NOTES

• • •

PLANT NAME:

SUNLIGHT

LEVEL OF SUNLIGHT:
○ LOW ◐ BRIGHT / INDIRECT ◑ PARTIAL / DIRECT ● DIRECT

THRIVES IN THIS LOCATION: _____
_____
_____

WATER

AMOUNT:
☐ LET DRY OUT ☐ MIST ☐ KEEP DAMP ☐ SOAK

FREQUENCY:
☐ 2–3X WEEK ☐ 1–2X WEEK ☐ WEEKLY ☐ BI-WEEKLY ☐ MONTHLY

WATER ON:
☐ MON ☐ TUE ☐ WED ☐ THU ☐ FRI ☐ SAT ☐ SUN

SOIL

TYPE OF SOIL: _____
_____
_____

PREFERRED BRAND: _____
_____

FERTILIZER

TYPE OF FERTILIZER: _____
_____

PREFERRED BRAND: _____
_____

FREQUENCY OF USE: _____

ADDITIONAL CARE NOTES

• • •

PLANT LOG

PLANT NAME:

SUNLIGHT

LEVEL OF SUNLIGHT:
○ LOW ◐ BRIGHT / INDIRECT ◐ PARTIAL / DIRECT ● DIRECT

THRIVES IN THIS LOCATION: _____

_____

_____

WATER

AMOUNT:
☐ LET DRY OUT ☐ MIST ☐ KEEP DAMP ☐ SOAK

FREQUENCY:
☐ 2–3X WEEK ☐ 1–2X WEEK ☐ WEEKLY ☐ BI-WEEKLY ☐ MONTHLY

WATER ON:
☐ MON ☐ TUE ☐ WED ☐ THU ☐ FRI ☐ SAT ☐ SUN

SOIL

TYPE OF SOIL: _____

_____

_____

PREFERRED BRAND: _____

_____

FERTILIZER

TYPE OF FERTILIZER: _____

_____

PREFERRED BRAND: _____

_____

FREQUENCY OF USE: _____

ADDITIONAL CARE NOTES

· · ·

PLANT NAME:

SUNLIGHT

LEVEL OF SUNLIGHT:
○ LOW ◑ BRIGHT / INDIRECT ◐ PARTIAL / DIRECT ● DIRECT

THRIVES IN THIS LOCATION: _____

_____

_____

WATER

AMOUNT:
☐ LET DRY OUT ☐ MIST ☐ KEEP DAMP ☐ SOAK

FREQUENCY:
☐ 2–3X WEEK ☐ 1–2X WEEK ☐ WEEKLY ☐ BI-WEEKLY ☐ MONTHLY

WATER ON:
☐ MON ☐ TUE ☐ WED ☐ THU ☐ FRI ☐ SAT ☐ SUN

SOIL

TYPE OF SOIL: _____

_____

_____

PREFERRED BRAND: _____

_____

FERTILIZER

TYPE OF FERTILIZER: _____

PREFERRED BRAND: _____

_____

FREQUENCY OF USE: _____

ADDITIONAL CARE NOTES

_____

_____

_____

_____

_____

_____

_____

_____

_____

_____

_____

_____

_____

_____

_____

_____

_____

_____

_____

• • •

PLANT NAME:

SUNLIGHT

LEVEL OF SUNLIGHT:
○ LOW ◐ BRIGHT / INDIRECT ◐ PARTIAL / DIRECT ● DIRECT

THRIVES IN THIS LOCATION: _____
_____
_____

WATER

AMOUNT:
☐ LET DRY OUT ☐ MIST ☐ KEEP DAMP ☐ SOAK

FREQUENCY:
☐ 2–3X WEEK ☐ 1–2X WEEK ☐ WEEKLY ☐ BI-WEEKLY ☐ MONTHLY

WATER ON:
☐ MON ☐ TUE ☐ WED ☐ THU ☐ FRI ☐ SAT ☐ SUN

SOIL

TYPE OF SOIL: _____
_____

PREFERRED BRAND: _____
_____

FERTILIZER

TYPE OF FERTILIZER: _____

PREFERRED BRAND: _____
_____

FREQUENCY OF USE: _____

ADDITIONAL CARE NOTES

• • •

PLANT NAME: _____

SUNLIGHT

LEVEL OF SUNLIGHT:
○ LOW ◐ BRIGHT / INDIRECT ◑ PARTIAL / DIRECT ● DIRECT

THRIVES IN THIS LOCATION: _____
_____
_____

WATER

AMOUNT:
☐ LET DRY OUT ☐ MIST ☐ KEEP DAMP ☐ SOAK

FREQUENCY:
☐ 2–3X WEEK ☐ 1–2X WEEK ☐ WEEKLY ☐ BI-WEEKLY ☐ MONTHLY

WATER ON:
☐ MON ☐ TUE ☐ WED ☐ THU ☐ FRI ☐ SAT ☐ SUN

SOIL

TYPE OF SOIL: _____
_____

PREFERRED BRAND: _____
_____

FERTILIZER

TYPE OF FERTILIZER: _____

PREFERRED BRAND: _____
_____

FREQUENCY OF USE: _____

ADDITIONAL CARE NOTES

· · ·

PLANT NAME:

SUNLIGHT

LEVEL OF SUNLIGHT:
○ LOW ◑ BRIGHT / INDIRECT ◑ PARTIAL / DIRECT ● DIRECT

THRIVES IN THIS LOCATION: _____
_____
_____

WATER

AMOUNT:
☐ LET DRY OUT ☐ MIST ☐ KEEP DAMP ☐ SOAK

FREQUENCY:
☐ 2–3X WEEK ☐ 1–2X WEEK ☐ WEEKLY ☐ BI-WEEKLY ☐ MONTHLY

WATER ON:
☐ MON ☐ TUE ☐ WED ☐ THU ☐ FRI ☐ SAT ☐ SUN

SOIL

TYPE OF SOIL: _____
_____

PREFERRED BRAND: _____
_____

FERTILIZER

TYPE OF FERTILIZER: _____

PREFERRED BRAND: _____

FREQUENCY OF USE: _____

ADDITIONAL CARE NOTES

...

PLANT NAME:

SUNLIGHT

LEVEL OF SUNLIGHT:
○ LOW ◐ BRIGHT / INDIRECT ◑ PARTIAL / DIRECT ● DIRECT

THRIVES IN THIS LOCATION: _____

_____

_____

WATER

AMOUNT:
☐ LET DRY OUT ☐ MIST ☐ KEEP DAMP ☐ SOAK

FREQUENCY:
☐ 2–3X WEEK ☐ 1–2X WEEK ☐ WEEKLY ☐ BI-WEEKLY ☐ MONTHLY

WATER ON:
☐ MON ☐ TUE ☐ WED ☐ THU ☐ FRI ☐ SAT ☐ SUN

SOIL

TYPE OF SOIL: _____

_____

_____

PREFERRED BRAND: _____

_____

FERTILIZER

TYPE OF FERTILIZER: _____

_____

PREFERRED BRAND: _____

_____

FREQUENCY OF USE: _____

ADDITIONAL CARE NOTES

• • •

PLANT NAME: _____

SUNLIGHT

LEVEL OF SUNLIGHT:
○ LOW ◐ BRIGHT / INDIRECT ◑ PARTIAL / DIRECT ● DIRECT

THRIVES IN THIS LOCATION: _____
_____
_____

WATER

AMOUNT:
☐ LET DRY OUT ☐ MIST ☐ KEEP DAMP ☐ SOAK

FREQUENCY:
☐ 2–3X WEEK ☐ 1–2X WEEK ☐ WEEKLY ☐ BI-WEEKLY ☐ MONTHLY

WATER ON:
☐ MON ☐ TUE ☐ WED ☐ THU ☐ FRI ☐ SAT ☐ SUN

SOIL

TYPE OF SOIL: _____
_____
_____

PREFERRED BRAND: _____
_____

FERTILIZER

TYPE OF FERTILIZER: _____
_____

PREFERRED BRAND: _____
_____

FREQUENCY OF USE: _____

ADDITIONAL CARE NOTES

_____

_____

_____

_____

_____

_____

_____

_____

_____

_____

_____

_____

_____

_____

_____

_____

_____

_____

_____

_____

• • •

PLANT NAME: _____

SUNLIGHT

LEVEL OF SUNLIGHT:
○ LOW ◐ BRIGHT / INDIRECT ◑ PARTIAL / DIRECT ● DIRECT

THRIVES IN THIS LOCATION: _____

_____

_____

WATER

AMOUNT:
☐ LET DRY OUT ☐ MIST ☐ KEEP DAMP ☐ SOAK

FREQUENCY:
☐ 2–3X WEEK ☐ 1–2X WEEK ☐ WEEKLY ☐ BI-WEEKLY ☐ MONTHLY

WATER ON:
☐ MON ☐ TUE ☐ WED ☐ THU ☐ FRI ☐ SAT ☐ SUN

SOIL

TYPE OF SOIL: _____

_____

_____

PREFERRED BRAND: _____

_____

FERTILIZER

TYPE OF FERTILIZER: _____

_____

PREFERRED BRAND: _____

_____

FREQUENCY OF USE: _____

ADDITIONAL CARE NOTES

_____

_____

_____

_____

_____

_____

_____

_____

_____

_____

_____

_____

_____

_____

_____

_____

_____

_____

_____

_____

_____

_____

_____

_____

• • •

• • •

· · ·

· · ·

・・・

• • •

• • •

OUTDOOR
PLANTS

Geraniums

Geraniums (*Geranium*) are popular flowering plants for hanging baskets, both indoors and outdoors, and they're often used in flower beds as well. They're easy to care for, and add a bright splash of color to any space. Native to South Africa, geraniums come in a range of

colors, including white, purple, pink, red, and orange. There are many different species of geraniums, so you have a wide array of colors, sizes, and leaf shapes to choose from.

LIGHT

Geraniums love the sun. They prefer to get at least six hours of full sunlight a day, although depending on how hot the environment is, they may need some amount of shade during the hottest part of the day.

WATER +SOIL

You should allow the soil to dry out before watering again. Make sure to use well-draining soil to avoid root rot.

OTHER INFO

Geraniums are prone to fungal infections and leaf spots, so you should make sure there's enough air circulation around the plants to prevent these kinds of problems. You should also be sure to remove any damaged leaves or stems so the disease or infection doesn't spread.

Lavender

Lavender (*Lavandula*) is a fragrant plant with distinctive violet-colored flowers, native to parts of Europe and northern Africa. It's commonly used in cosmetics, essential oils, and perfumes. Many people believe that lavender has calming effects, and some claim that it helps with problems such as sleeplessness, anxiety, and depression.

LIGHT

Lavender grows best in full sun, preferring six to eight hours a day of sun. In very hot areas, some shade may be necessary during the hottest parts of the day.

WATER +SOIL

Use a moderately fertile, well-draining soil. Lavender should be watered once or twice a week just after it's planted, but be wary of overwatering once the plant is established.

OTHER INFO

Lavender can be used to attract pollinators, such as butterflies and bees. It does best if planted in the spring, but it can be planted in the fall as well.

Mint

Used mainly as a culinary herb, mint (*Mentha*) is a perennial plant with a distinctive smell and taste. Mint is a great plant for beginners because it grows quickly, is easy to take care of, and can be used to season a wide range of foods. Try using mint leaves to make your own mint tea—or even mint chip ice cream!

LIGHT

Mint likes the sun, although it can survive in some shade. Like many plants, in very hot areas it may need some protection from the sun during the hottest parts of the day.

WATER +SOIL

Mint prefers to be in a moist environment, but you should still use well-draining soil.

OTHER INFO

Mint is a fast-growing plant, and it spreads very easily. It can take over your garden if left to its own devices, so make sure to keep an eye on it and remove any plants you don't need or want as soon as they grow.

Basil

Basil (*Ocimum basilicum*) is an herb in the mint family. It is a very common and popular seasoning, making it a useful plant to add to your garden or windowsill. Native to tropical areas of Africa and Asia, it only grows in the summer, when the soil is sufficiently warm.

LIGHT | Basil likes a lot of sunlight—a minimum of six to eight hours a day.

WATER +SOIL | Basil prefers to be in a moist environment, but you should still use well-draining soil.

OTHER INFO | If you eat a lot of pesto, it's worth your while to add basil to your garden, because basil is one of the key ingredients in that sauce. Just make sure that the soil is clean if you're planning to use basil as a cooking ingredient.

Daylilies

Daylilies (*Hemerocallis*) are flowering perennial plants native to eastern Asia. They're a popular plant for gardens because of their beautiful, colorful flowers. They're also popular because of their longevity—if properly cared for, they can last for many years.

LIGHT

Daylilies prefer to get at least six hours of full sun a day. Like many other flowering plants and herbs, depending on how hot it gets, they may need some shade during the sunniest parts of the day.

WATER +SOIL

Daylilies like to be in a moist environment, but the soil should still be well-draining to avoid rot and mold.

OTHER INFO

Daylilies only last for one day; they open in the morning and die at night. The name *Hemerocallis* comes from the Greek words for "day" and "beautiful." Luckily, most stems have multiple buds, and each plant has multiple stems, so daylily plants can produce many flowers. One downside to daylilies is that they're toxic to cats.

COMMON PROBLEMS WITH OUTDOOR PLANTS

Insects. Insects and pests are a very common cause of death for both indoor and outdoor plants. Some of the most common kinds of insects and pests are mealybugs, scale insects, whiteflies, and spider mites. All plants are susceptible to insects and pests, but poor conditions (too much or too little water or light, for instance), will increase the likelihood of pests. To avoid insects and pests, make sure you're watering your plants properly and providing the right temperature, humidity, and light conditions. If you do see signs of insect activity, you should wipe off the plant as soon as possible. You may have to use an insecticidal spray as well. Unfortunately, if the infestation is bad, you may need to get rid of the plant, especially if you have other plants nearby, because an infestation can spread from one plant to another.

Frost/cold. Outdoor plants are easily damaged by frost and cold temperatures. If you know the temperature is going to be unseasonably cold, you should cover your outdoor plants with a plastic sheet or a cloth to prevent damage.

Poor soil conditions. If a plant doesn't get enough nutrients, it can start to wilt, and if the problem isn't corrected, it may even die. Different plants prefer different kinds of soil, so you should make sure that you use the right kind of soil for each plant. If your plants are in containers, make sure to repot them every so often with fresh soil to keep them healthy—and always repot a plant if it has become root bound.

Yellowing leaves. Leaves can start to turn yellow for many reasons, including overwatering, underwatering, pests, heat, cold, or lack of nutrients. Unfortunately, it's often hard to tell why a plant has yellowing leaves. If the soil is very dry, it's likely that you aren't giving your plant enough water. If the soil is always damp or wet, you may be giving your plant too much water. Check for pests by looking for any other irregularities on the leaves or stems. Check that the temperature and humidity levels are appropriate for each plant. If the plant hasn't been fertilized in a long time, it may be that it needs nutrients, so you could try fertilizing the soil.

Wilting. Plants can wilt for a wide range of reasons, including too little water, too much sun, and pests or diseases. They can also wilt if they're root bound, meaning their roots don't have room to expand and seek nutrients, or if they're over fertilized. The most common cause of wilting is lack of water, so you should check first to make sure that your plant is getting sufficient water.

KEEPING TRACK OF YOUR OUTDOOR PLANTS

Once you select the plants that will be putting down roots in your garden—whether the ones described here or your own favorites—it's important to keep track of the conditions that help them blossom! In the pages that follow you'll find pages to log important factors, like preferred amounts of sunlight and watering schedules, as well as space to record your observations and tips you might pick up from friends. Here are some questions and topics to keep in mind as you get to know your plant companions:

Does this plant grow best in the ground, a raised bed, or a container?

....

When is the best time to plant?

....

Is there a flowering period or a time for harvesting fruits/vegetables?

....

What are the best practices for pruning this plant?

....

How should I prep for overwintering?

PLANT NAME:

SUNLIGHT

LEVEL OF SUNLIGHT:
○ LOW ◐ PART ● FULL

THRIVES WHEN FACING:
☐ NORTH ☐ SOUTH ☐ EAST ☐ WEST

WATER

FREQUENCY:
☐ WEEKLY ☐ 2–3X WEEK ☐ DAILY ☐ 2X DAILY

WATER ON:
☐ MON ☐ TUE ☐ WED ☐ THU ☐ FRI ☐ SAT ☐ SUN

SOIL

TYPE OF SOIL: _____

_____

_____

PREFERRED BRAND: _____

_____

FERTILIZER

TYPE OF FERTILIZER: _____

PREFERRED BRAND: _____

_____

FREQUENCY OF USE: _____

ADDITIONAL CARE NOTES

_____
_____
_____
_____
_____
_____
_____
_____
_____
_____
_____
_____
_____
_____
_____
_____
_____
_____
_____
_____
_____
_____
_____
_____
_____

• • •

PLANT LOG

PLANT NAME:

SUNLIGHT

LEVEL OF SUNLIGHT:
○ LOW ◑ PART ● FULL

THRIVES WHEN FACING:
☐ NORTH ☐ SOUTH ☐ EAST ☐ WEST

WATER

FREQUENCY:
☐ WEEKLY ☐ 2–3X WEEK ☐ DAILY ☐ 2X DAILY

WATER ON:
☐ MON ☐ TUE ☐ WED ☐ THU ☐ FRI ☐ SAT ☐ SUN

SOIL

TYPE OF SOIL: _____

_____

PREFERRED BRAND: _____

_____

FERTILIZER

TYPE OF FERTILIZER: _____

PREFERRED BRAND: _____

FREQUENCY OF USE: _____

ADDITIONAL CARE NOTES

• • •

PLANT NAME:

SUNLIGHT

LEVEL OF SUNLIGHT:
○ LOW ◐ PART ● FULL

THRIVES WHEN FACING:
☐ NORTH ☐ SOUTH ☐ EAST ☐ WEST

WATER

FREQUENCY:
☐ WEEKLY ☐ 2–3X WEEK ☐ DAILY ☐ 2X DAILY

WATER ON:
☐ MON ☐ TUE ☐ WED ☐ THU ☐ FRI ☐ SAT ☐ SUN

SOIL

TYPE OF SOIL: _____
_____
_____

PREFERRED BRAND: _____
_____

FERTILIZER

TYPE OF FERTILIZER: _____
_____

PREFERRED BRAND: _____
_____

FREQUENCY OF USE: _____

ADDITIONAL CARE NOTES

- - -

PLANT NAME:

SUNLIGHT

LEVEL OF SUNLIGHT:
○ LOW ◑ PART ● FULL

THRIVES WHEN FACING:
☐ NORTH ☐ SOUTH ☐ EAST ☐ WEST

WATER

FREQUENCY:
☐ WEEKLY ☐ 2–3X WEEK ☐ DAILY ☐ 2X DAILY

WATER ON:
☐ MON ☐ TUE ☐ WED ☐ THU ☐ FRI ☐ SAT ☐ SUN

SOIL

TYPE OF SOIL: _____
_____
_____

PREFERRED BRAND: _____
_____

FERTILIZER

TYPE OF FERTILIZER: _____
_____

PREFERRED BRAND: _____
_____

FREQUENCY OF USE: _____

ADDITIONAL CARE NOTES

• • •

PLANT NAME:

SUNLIGHT

LEVEL OF SUNLIGHT:
○ LOW ◑ PART ● FULL

THRIVES WHEN FACING:
☐ NORTH ☐ SOUTH ☐ EAST ☐ WEST

WATER

FREQUENCY:
☐ WEEKLY ☐ 2–3X WEEK ☐ DAILY ☐ 2X DAILY

WATER ON:
☐ MON ☐ TUE ☐ WED ☐ THU ☐ FRI ☐ SAT ☐ SUN

SOIL

TYPE OF SOIL: _____

_____

_____

PREFERRED BRAND: _____

_____

FERTILIZER

TYPE OF FERTILIZER: _____

_____

PREFERRED BRAND: _____

_____

FREQUENCY OF USE: _____

ADDITIONAL CARE NOTES

. . .

PLANT NAME:

SUNLIGHT

LEVEL OF SUNLIGHT:
◯ LOW ◗ PART ● FULL

THRIVES WHEN FACING:
☐ NORTH ☐ SOUTH ☐ EAST ☐ WEST

WATER

FREQUENCY:
☐ WEEKLY ☐ 2–3X WEEK ☐ DAILY ☐ 2X DAILY

WATER ON:
☐ MON ☐ TUE ☐ WED ☐ THU ☐ FRI ☐ SAT ☐ SUN

SOIL

TYPE OF SOIL: _____
_____
_____

PREFERRED BRAND: _____
_____

FERTILIZER

TYPE OF FERTILIZER: _____

PREFERRED BRAND: _____
_____

FREQUENCY OF USE: _____

ADDITIONAL CARE NOTES

• • •

PLANT NAME:

SUNLIGHT

LEVEL OF SUNLIGHT:
○ LOW ◑ PART ● FULL
THRIVES WHEN FACING:
☐ NORTH ☐ SOUTH ☐ EAST ☐ WEST

WATER

FREQUENCY:
☐ WEEKLY ☐ 2–3X WEEK ☐ DAILY ☐ 2X DAILY
WATER ON:
☐ MON ☐ TUE ☐ WED ☐ THU ☐ FRI ☐ SAT ☐ SUN

SOIL

TYPE OF SOIL: _____

_____

_____

PREFERRED BRAND: _____

_____

FERTILIZER

TYPE OF FERTILIZER: _____

_____

PREFERRED BRAND: _____

_____

FREQUENCY OF USE: _____

ADDITIONAL CARE NOTES

_____
_____
_____
_____
_____
_____
_____
_____
_____
_____
_____
_____
_____
_____
_____
_____
_____
_____
_____
_____
_____

• • •

PLANT NAME:

SUNLIGHT

LEVEL OF SUNLIGHT:
○ LOW ◐ PART ● FULL

THRIVES WHEN FACING:
☐ NORTH ☐ SOUTH ☐ EAST ☐ WEST

WATER

FREQUENCY:
☐ WEEKLY ☐ 2–3X WEEK ☐ DAILY ☐ 2X DAILY

WATER ON:
☐ MON ☐ TUE ☐ WED ☐ THU ☐ FRI ☐ SAT ☐ SUN

SOIL

TYPE OF SOIL: _____

_____

_____

PREFERRED BRAND: _____

_____

FERTILIZER

TYPE OF FERTILIZER: _____

PREFERRED BRAND: _____

FREQUENCY OF USE: _____

ADDITIONAL CARE NOTES

_____
_____
_____
_____
_____
_____
_____
_____
_____
_____
_____
_____
_____
_____
_____
_____
_____
_____
_____
_____
_____
_____
_____

• • •

PLANT NAME:

SUNLIGHT

LEVEL OF SUNLIGHT:
○ LOW ◑ PART ● FULL

THRIVES WHEN FACING:
☐ NORTH ☐ SOUTH ☐ EAST ☐ WEST

WATER

FREQUENCY:
☐ WEEKLY ☐ 2–3X WEEK ☐ DAILY ☐ 2X DAILY

WATER ON:
☐ MON ☐ TUE ☐ WED ☐ THU ☐ FRI ☐ SAT ☐ SUN

SOIL

TYPE OF SOIL: _____
_____
_____

PREFERRED BRAND: _____
_____

FERTILIZER

TYPE OF FERTILIZER: _____
_____

PREFERRED BRAND: _____
_____

FREQUENCY OF USE: _____

ADDITIONAL CARE NOTES

_____

_____

_____

_____

_____

_____

_____

_____

_____

_____

_____

_____

_____

_____

_____

_____

_____

_____

_____

_____

_____

_____

_____

• • •

PLANT NAME:

SUNLIGHT

LEVEL OF SUNLIGHT:
○ LOW ◐ PART ● FULL

THRIVES WHEN FACING:
☐ NORTH ☐ SOUTH ☐ EAST ☐ WEST

WATER

FREQUENCY:
☐ WEEKLY ☐ 2–3X WEEK ☐ DAILY ☐ 2X DAILY

WATER ON:
☐ MON ☐ TUE ☐ WED ☐ THU ☐ FRI ☐ SAT ☐ SUN

SOIL

TYPE OF SOIL: _____

_____

_____

PREFERRED BRAND: _____

FERTILIZER

TYPE OF FERTILIZER: _____

_____

PREFERRED BRAND: _____

_____

FREQUENCY OF USE: _____

ADDITIONAL CARE NOTES

_____

_____

_____

_____

_____

_____

_____

_____

_____

_____

_____

_____

_____

_____

_____

_____

_____

_____

_____

_____

_____

_____

• • •

PLANT NAME:

SUNLIGHT

LEVEL OF SUNLIGHT:
○ LOW ◑ PART ● FULL

THRIVES WHEN FACING:
☐ NORTH ☐ SOUTH ☐ EAST ☐ WEST

WATER

FREQUENCY:
☐ WEEKLY ☐ 2–3X WEEK ☐ DAILY ☐ 2X DAILY

WATER ON:
☐ MON ☐ TUE ☐ WED ☐ THU ☐ FRI ☐ SAT ☐ SUN

SOIL

TYPE OF SOIL: _____

_____

_____

PREFERRED BRAND: _____

_____

FERTILIZER

TYPE OF FERTILIZER: _____

PREFERRED BRAND: _____

FREQUENCY OF USE: _____

ADDITIONAL CARE NOTES

_____
_____
_____
_____
_____
_____
_____
_____
_____
_____
_____
_____
_____
_____
_____
_____
_____
_____
_____
_____

• • •

PLANT LOG

PLANT NAME:

SUNLIGHT

LEVEL OF SUNLIGHT:
○ LOW ◑ PART ● FULL

THRIVES WHEN FACING:
☐ NORTH ☐ SOUTH ☐ EAST ☐ WEST

WATER

FREQUENCY:
☐ WEEKLY ☐ 2–3X WEEK ☐ DAILY ☐ 2X DAILY

WATER ON:
☐ MON ☐ TUE ☐ WED ☐ THU ☐ FRI ☐ SAT ☐ SUN

SOIL

TYPE OF SOIL: _____

_____

_____

PREFERRED BRAND: _____

_____

FERTILIZER

TYPE OF FERTILIZER: _____

PREFERRED BRAND: _____

_____

FREQUENCY OF USE: _____

ADDITIONAL CARE NOTES

_____
_____
_____
_____
_____
_____
_____
_____
_____
_____
_____
_____
_____
_____
_____
_____
_____
_____
_____
_____
_____

• • •

PLANT NAME:

SUNLIGHT

LEVEL OF SUNLIGHT:
○ LOW ◑ PART ● FULL

THRIVES WHEN FACING:
☐ NORTH ☐ SOUTH ☐ EAST ☐ WEST

WATER

FREQUENCY:
☐ WEEKLY ☐ 2–3X WEEK ☐ DAILY ☐ 2X DAILY

WATER ON:
☐ MON ☐ TUE ☐ WED ☐ THU ☐ FRI ☐ SAT ☐ SUN

SOIL

TYPE OF SOIL: _____

_____

_____

PREFERRED BRAND: _____

_____

FERTILIZER

TYPE OF FERTILIZER: _____

_____

PREFERRED BRAND: _____

_____

FREQUENCY OF USE: _____

ADDITIONAL CARE NOTES

_____

_____

_____

_____

_____

_____

_____

_____

_____

_____

_____

_____

_____

_____

_____

_____

_____

_____

_____

_____

_____

_____

• • •

PLANT NAME:

SUNLIGHT

LEVEL OF SUNLIGHT:
○ LOW ◑ PART ● FULL

THRIVES WHEN FACING:
☐ NORTH ☐ SOUTH ☐ EAST ☐ WEST

WATER

FREQUENCY:
☐ WEEKLY ☐ 2–3X WEEK ☐ DAILY ☐ 2X DAILY

WATER ON:
☐ MON ☐ TUE ☐ WED ☐ THU ☐ FRI ☐ SAT ☐ SUN

SOIL

TYPE OF SOIL: _____

_____

PREFERRED BRAND: _____

_____

FERTILIZER

TYPE OF FERTILIZER: _____

PREFERRED BRAND: _____

_____

FREQUENCY OF USE: _____

ADDITIONAL CARE NOTES

_____
_____
_____
_____
_____
_____
_____
_____
_____
_____
_____
_____
_____
_____
_____
_____
_____
_____
_____
_____
_____
_____

. . .

PLANT NAME:

SUNLIGHT

LEVEL OF SUNLIGHT:
○ LOW ◑ PART ● FULL
THRIVES WHEN FACING:
☐ NORTH ☐ SOUTH ☐ EAST ☐ WEST

WATER

FREQUENCY:
☐ WEEKLY ☐ 2–3X WEEK ☐ DAILY ☐ 2X DAILY
WATER ON:
☐ MON ☐ TUE ☐ WED ☐ THU ☐ FRI ☐ SAT ☐ SUN

SOIL

TYPE OF SOIL: _____
_____
_____
PREFERRED BRAND: _____
_____

FERTILIZER

TYPE OF FERTILIZER: _____
PREFERRED BRAND: _____
_____
FREQUENCY OF USE: _____

PLANT LOG

ADDITIONAL CARE NOTES

• • •

・・・

• • •

・・・

• • •

・・・

* * *

• • •

· · ·

PLANT
DREAMS

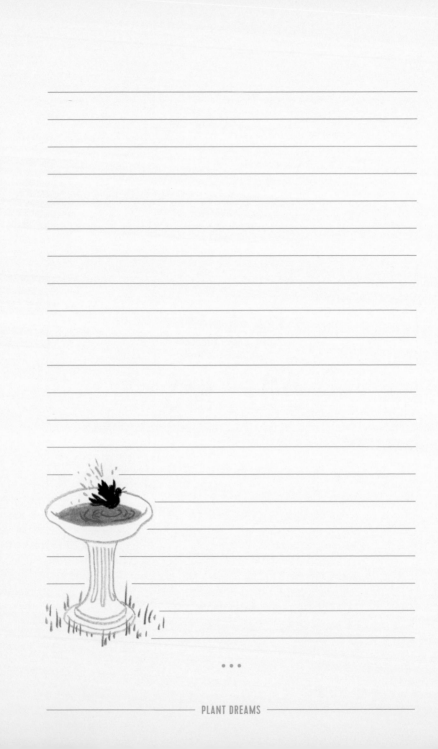

· · ·

· · ·

• • •

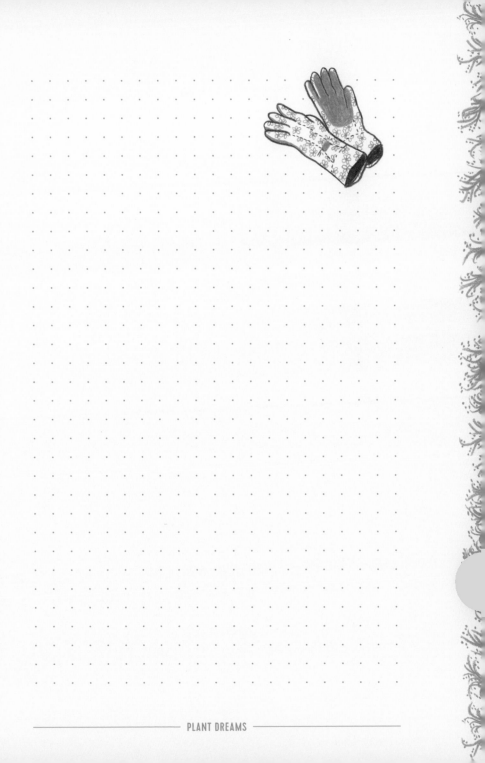

●●●

• • •

· · ·

・・・

• • •

· · ·

• • •

• • •